THE WOMEN OF
1883

Royce Preston Rolland

D1526200

**HELLO
CARLO
PRESS**

THE WOMEN OF
1883

INTRODUCTION

There's a little show called YELLOWSTONE starring Kevin Costner that debuted on the Paramount network on June 20, 2018. Four plus years later, it is about to be enter its 5th season at the time of this writing. Costner plays the role of JOHN DUTTON III, a 6th generation patriarch of the DUTTON FAMILY who is a cattle rancher and operates the Yellowstone Dutton Ranch in Montana. 1883 tells the story of his grandfather's grandparents, who departed from Tennessee and headed west to Texas before heading north where they eventually ended up in Montana. The grandfather's grandparents are JAMES DUTTON and MARGARET DUTTON (played by Tim McGraw and Faith Hill).

JAMES was a captain in the Confederate States Army during

the Civil War. At the Battle of Antietam in 1862, he was wounded in battle and captured. He was held in a union prisoner-of-war camp for three years.

After the war's end in May 1865, he and his wife soon had daughter ELSA, born on April 9, 1866, and about 12 years later they had another child, JOHN.

1883 in Fort Worth, Texas is portrayed as quite a hostile place. The Dutton family experienced a fair amount of tragedy on their journey from Texas to Montana. In an alternate universe, perhaps they could have made their way via train from Tennessee to Omaha, Nebraska and onward to Ogden, Utah in 1883 and spared themselves some of the pain and suffering.

1883 was an interesting watch, seasoned with fantastic

performances, excellent writing, and wonderful scenery. Another Yellowstone spinoff entitled 1923, 40 years after the events of 1883 is set to debut in December 2022. The show's leads will be Harrison Ford and Helen Mirren. Ford will play the role of JACOB DUTTON (brother of JAMES DUTTON, played by Tim McGraw) and Mirren plays his wife CARA DUTTON.

Isabel May and Faith Hill turn in outstanding performances as mother and daughter in 1883. The final moments of Dawn Olivieri's performance as CLAIRE in episode 2 was both powerful and heartbreaking.

Thank you for reading.....

-RPR, November 2022

LIST OF
EPISODES
1-10

"1883"

"BEHIND US, A CLIFF"

E3.

"RIVER"

E4.

"THE CROSSING"

"RACING CLOUDS"

"THIS IS NOT YOUR HEAVEN"

INDEX OF CREDITED AND UNCREDITED ACTRESSES

AMANDA
FURMAN

GYPSY EMIGRANT
(UNCREDITED)
(EP 3-5)

AMANDA
JAROS

ALINA
(EP 1-9)

NOTE:
An immigrant wife, she trades with
ELSA.

AMBER BLAZE LAMMOND

SLAVIC EMIGRANT
(EP 2)

SLAVIC EMIGRANT
(UNCREDITED)
(EP 4 & 5)

ANNA
FIAMORA

RISA
(EP 1-10)

NOTE:
Wife of JOSEF, the interpreter.

ASLAN TUDOR

COMANCHE TEEN
(UNCREDITED)
(EP 8)

BRYNLEE NOWLIN

RAVI'S DAUGHTER
(UNCREDITED)
(EP 5)

CANDICE
FAITH
KNIGHT

PROSTITUTE
(UNCREDITED)
(EP 1)

CASSIDY
AURORA
GORDON

SMALLPOX
MAN'S WIFE
(EP 1)

CHRISTINA GONZALEZ

COACH
TRAIN PASSENGER
(UNCREDITED)
(EP 1)

COURTNEY
HERBST

SMILTE
(EP 2)

DAWN M. HITT

GERMAN EMIGRANT
(UNCREDITED)
(EP 1-5)

DAWN
OLIVIERI

CLAIRE
(EP 1 & 2)

NOTE:
Sister of JAMES; mother of MARY
ABEL; recently widowed and
commits suicide at the grave of her
daughter and last surviving child
MARY ABEL.

DAWSYN
EUBANKS

YOUNG WOMAN
SNAKE BITE
(EP 3)

EMMA
MALOUFF

MARY ABEL
(EP 1 & 2)

NOTE:
Daughter of CLAIRE; gets caught in a crossfire and dies from a bullet wound. Her grave is near the river where they established camp.

FAITH
HILL

MARGARET DUTTON
(EP 1-10)

NOTE:
Wife of JAMES; mother of ELSA and
JOHN.
Great-great-grandmother of JOHN
DUTTON III (Kevin Costner's
character in YELLOWSTONE).
She is the grandmother of JOHN
DUTTON III's grandfather.

GILI SAGE GOULD

GERMAN
EMIGRANT GIRL
(UNCREDITED)
(EP 1-5, 7-8)

GINA
BARTON
SEWELL

TRAVELLER
(UNCREDITED)
(EP 1)

GRATIELA BRANCUSI

NOEMI
(EP 1-10)

NOTE:
A recently widowed Romani woman
with two sons, she starts a romance
with THOMAS.

ISABEL

MAY

ELSA DUTTON
(EP 1-10)

NOTE:
17-year-old-daughter of JAMES and
MARGARET DUTTON; sister of 5-
year-old JOHN DUTTON.

JAYDEN HAMILTON

GERMAN EMIGRANT
(UNCREDITED)
(EP 1-5, 7-9)

JESSICA
SWINNEY

GERMAN EMIGRANT
(UNCREDITED)
(EP 1-8)

JOANNA DeLANE

CLOTHES MAKER
(EP 8)

KATHERINE
HOGAN

FIRST CLASS
TRAIN PASSENGER
(UNCREDITED)
(EP 1)

LAUREN
MARIE
GORDON

TRAIN PASSENGER
(UNCREDITED)
(EP 1)

LEANNE
BRUISED
HEAD

CROW WOMAN #1
(EP 10)

LILLIANA
VITTORIA
APONTE
MORENO

SINGER
(EP 2)

LINDSEY
ROBERTS

THIRD CLASS
TRAIN PASSENGER
(EP 1)

LYUBA
ROSE

SORINA
(EP 2,8)

MACKINLEE WADDELL

YOUNG WOMAN
(EP 1)

MADISON BOWLING

ALLEY WOMAN
(EP 1)

MELISSA
LADD

SHEA'S WIFE
(EP 1)

MELISSA
SELLERS-
DURHAM

COMANCHE WOMAN
(UNCREDITED)
(EP 8)

MIKAELA
FREE

GERMAN EMIGRANT
(UNCREDITED)
(EP 1-5)

MORGAN LESTER

YOUNG COMANCHE WOMAN
WOMAN
(EP 8)

NATALIE DICKINSON

SHEA'S DAUGHTER
(EP 1)

NICHOLE GALICIA

STREET LADY (UNCREDITED) (EP 1)

PAMELA MITCHELL

RED DRESS
(EP 1 & 2)

PATTI
BRINDLEY

COWGIRL
(EP 1 & 2)

RACHEL
HEPTNER

WICHTE
(EP 2 & 3)

RITA
WILSON

CAROLYN
(EP 6)

NOTE:
A kind storekeeper at Doan's Crossing
at the border of Texas and Oklahoma.
When MARGARET DUTTON enters
store they become friendly and drink
whiskey together.

SARA
ACOSTA

GYPSY EMIGRANT
(UNCREDITED)
(EP 1-6)

SAVANNAH SOLSBERY

SHEA'S GRANDDAUGHTER (UNCREDITED) (EP 1)

SHANNA
TOFT

RUSSIAN EMIGRANT
(UNCREDITED)
(EP 1-7)

SHAYLA
BAGIR

SORINA
(EP 1)

SHAYNA
ADLER

PROSTITUTE
(UNCREDITED)
(EP 2)

SOPHIA
GAIDAROVA

PIONEER CHILD #2
(EP 8)

STEPHANIE

NUR

MELODI
(EP 1 & 2)

STEPHANIE
ST. PIERRE

PROSTITUTE
(UNCREDITED)
(EP 1)

COMANCHE WOMAN
(UNCREDITED)
(EP 8)

STORMY
STANFORD

EASTERN
EUROPEAN KID
(UNCREDITED)
(EP 3)

TANA
STEWART

CROW WOMAN #2
(EP 10)

TRINITY
JOHNSON

RUSSIAN
EMIGRANT CHILD
(UNCREDITED)
(EP 4-7)

Made in the USA
Monee, IL
17 July 2023

39413323R00039